ART DECO TILES

Hans van Lemmen

SHIRE PUBLICATIONS

Published in Great Britain in 2012 by Shire Publications
Ltd, Midland House, West Way, Botley, Oxford OX2 0PH,
United Kingdom.

44-02 23rd Street, Suite 219, Long Island City, NY 11101,
USA.

E-mail: shire@shirebooks.co.uk   www.shirebooks.co.uk

A CIP catalogue record for this book is available from the
British Library.

Shire Library no. 705.   ISBN-13: 978 0 74781 199 2

Hans van Lemmen has asserted his right under the
Copyright, Designs and Patents Act, 1988, to be identified
as the author of this book.

Designed by Tony Truscott Designs, Sussex, UK
and typeset in Perpetua and Gill Sans.

Printed in China through Worldprint Ltd.

12 13 14 15 16   10 9 8 7 6 5 4 3 2 1

COVER IMAGE
Tube-lined tile with a semi-abstract streamlined seascape
and flying seagulls. Made by Carter & Co., 1935.

TITLE PAGE IMAGE
A bold abstract Art Deco tile made by Richards Tiles,
c. 1937.

CONTENTS PAGE IMAGE
Lunette above one of the windows on the Sidney Street
Estate in Somers Town, St Pancras, London, designed by
Gilbert Bayes, 1931, showing 'The Soldier and the
Princess'.

ACKNOWLEDGEMENTS
The author is grateful to Mario Baeck, Chris Blanchett,
Adrian Grater, Josep Pérez Camps, Angela and Barry
Corbett, Ulli Hamburg, Roger Hensman, Douglas van der
Horst, Chris Marsden, Lynn Pearson, Paul Rothery, Thelma
Shepley, Amy Smith, Richard Smith, Michael Spender,
and Jon Wilson for their assistance in various ways.

I would like to thank people who have allowed me to use
illustrations which are acknowledges as follows:

Mario Baeck, page 8; Chris Blanchett, pages 21, 29, 30
(bottom right), 32 (top), 33 (bottom) 35, 36, 37 (top and
bottom), 40 (top), 41 (bottom), 43 (top right), 45 (top),
55, 56, 57 (bottom), 60; Fielding Auctioneers Ltd, pages
34 (bottom right), 41 (top), 62 (bottom); Ulli Hamburg,
pages 31 (bottom left), 40 (bottom left and right); Roger
Hensman, front cover, pages 30 (top), 31 (top and bottom
right), 33 (bottom left), 34 (bottom left); Douglas van der
Horst, title page, page 42 (bottom); Museu de Ceràmica
de Manises, page 9 (top); Peter Scott Gallery, Lancaster
University, page 14 (top); Paul Rothery, pages 10, 17;
Salford Museum and Art Gallery, pages 24, 32 (bottom);
Shaws of Darwen, pages 42 (top), 48 (top); Amy Smith,
page 4.

All other images are from the author's collection of
photographs.

Shire Publications is supporting the Woodland Trust, the UK's leading woodland conservation charity, by funding the dedication of trees.

CONTENTS

INTRODUCTION

ART DECO is recognised as the leading design movement of the 1920s and 1930s and, as such, affected many aspects of art, design and architecture, including tiles and architectural faience. It superseded Art Nouveau, which was the dominant decorative style in Europe in the late nineteenth and early twentieth centuries. Notable characteristics of Art Nouveau had been its sinuous floral designs with complex interwoven patterns of stems, leaves and flowers, and its female figures with long streaming hair, but, although things were changing, it is not always easy to draw a clear dividing line between these two design movements. The roots of Art Deco were already discernible before the onset of the First World War (1914–18), and Art Deco can be seen both as a reaction to Art Nouveau and as a continuation of it.

The term 'Art Deco' comes from the important international design exhibition held in Paris in 1925 under the name *Exposition Internationale des Arts Décoratifs*. It ran for six months and was seen by over fifteen million people. Such international gatherings were important venues for the dissemination and exchange of new design ideas and this exhibition in particular was intended to give an overview of the best of the modern design produced by the industrialised nations of the post-war world. With the notable exceptions of Germany and the United States, many countries were represented. Not only did France, the host country, have a national pavilion, but notable French manufacturers such as Sèvres and fashionable Paris design stores such as Galeries Lafayette also had their own individual pavilions. The latter's pavilion was called '*La Maitrise*', where the latest French designs of the 1920s were on show, with an emphasis on elegance, hand-applied decoration and the use of expensive materials and processes. Visitors entered the pavilion by walking under a spectacular sunburst motif that was to become the iconic design symbol of Art Deco style. The British pavilion showed the wares of British manufacturers and craftsmen such as the ceramics manufacturer Carter & Co. However, during the inter-war period the term 'Art Deco' was not used, but the words 'modern' or the French '*moderne*' were used instead. The term 'Art Deco' was first used by the design critic Bevis Hillier in 1968,

Opposite:
The colourful tiled façade of the Paramount Theatre in Oakland, California, USA. Made by Gladding McBean, 1931.

5

in his book *Art Deco of the Twenties and Thirties*. This was followed by a ground-breaking exhibition at the Minneapolis Institute of Arts in the United States in 1971 called 'The World of Art Deco'. Since then Art Deco has become recognised as one of the most exciting and important episodes in the history of twentieth-century design, noted for its sleek aerodynamic lines, highly stylised figurative designs and bold colourful abstract patterns.

Art Deco was an eclectic style that drew on many different stylistic influences, such as European avant-garde (particularly the abstract art of painters such as Kandinsky, Malevich and Mondrian), classical architecture, the ancient civilisations of Egypt and South America and exotic cultures from the Far East. These myriad sources can also be seen in the design of tiles and architectural faience, but how this manifested itself varied greatly from country to country. Art Deco was a much more vehement design force on the continent of Europe and in the United States than in Britain, and, before examining what happened in Britain in more detail, it may be useful to look briefly at what was produced elsewhere by designers and manufacturers in the 1920s and 1930s.

In France, Art Deco tiles and faience were often characterised by stylised and elegant designs with much emphasis on hand-crafted forms and techniques. The firm Fourmaintraux in Desvres produced some interesting work of this kind. In the Netherlands there was a strong predilection for expressionist and exotic designs, of which the famous Tuschinski Theatre in

Postcard of the pavilion of the Galeries Lafayette at the *Exposition Internationale des Arts Décoratifs et Industriels Modernes* in Paris, 1925. It was one of the leading pavilions in the show, with a striking 'sunburst' motif over the entrance.

EXPOSITION INTERNATIONALE DES ARTS DÉCORATIFS — PARIS - 1925
PAVILLON «LA MAITRISE» Atelier des ARTS APPLIQUES des GALERIES LAFAYETTE
(par Jean Hiriart, Georges Tribout. et Georges Beau. architectes)   A. P

Amsterdam is a case in point. The faience decorations on the exterior of this building range from human and animal forms cowering under jagged thunderbolts, to ornamental features borrowed from Hindu temples in Indonesia, including elephants' heads. In Belgium the designer Joseph Roelants created some dazzling Art Deco tile panels for the firm Gilliot & Cie at Hemiksem, depicting subjects such as the Greek sun god Apollo descending from the heavens in a chariot, executed in gold and silver tiles. Even in Spain the Art Deco style

Tile-and-mosaic panel showing a stylised plant in a flowerpot in the Art Deco style on a shop front in Desvres, Pas-de-Calais, made by Fourmaintraux & Delassus in Desvres, c. 1925.

Detail of the Art Deco faience decorations on the façade of the famous Tuschinski Theatre in Amsterdam made by Plateelbakkerij Delft, Hilversum, Netherlands, in 1921. The exotic forms of the faience, glass and metal decorations are reminiscent of German Expressionism.

An exuberant Art Deco tile panel showing the sun god Apollo in his chariot, riding the heavens. Designed by the artist Joseph Roelants and made by Gilliot & Cie, Hemiksem, Belgium, 1935.

manifested itself often with typical southern exuberance. Tiled dados for the entrances of Spanish houses featured bright abstract designs and colours, augmented with cartoon characters suvh as Mickey Mouse, showing how the design of tiles could be influenced even by American film culture. During the 1920s and 1930s Art Deco was a very strong influence in the United States, where skyscrapers, office blocks, apartment blocks, theatres and cinemas were often decorated with a vast array of figurative or abstract tiles and

Tile panel made by Leopoldo Mora, Manises, Spain, c. 1935. The colourful Art Deco designs are augmented by tiles showing Walt Disney's Mickey Mouse.

Tile with an abstract hand-painted design, made by the American Encaustic Tiling Company in Zanesville, Ohio, USA, c. 1930. The black outlines and the bold use of blue and orange (complementary colours) make it a striking Art Deco tile.

architectural faience on a scale unseen in Europe. The Paramount Theatre in Oakland, California, with monumental Art Deco tiling made by the firm Gladding McBean, is a prime example of this trend.

J. & W. WADE & CO.
FLAXMAN TILE WORKS
BURSLEM, ENG.

Telegrams: "WADES, BURSLEM"
Telephone: 341
A.B.C. Code, 5th Edition

P 382x   P 381x   P 107A   P 171x   P 269A   P 154x   P 171C   P 107F   P 107H

P 272x   P 280x   P 97D   P 245x   P 130x   P 99x   P 103A   P 102x

P 99F   P 97A   P 237C   P 66C   P 69B   P 100B   P 99B   P 102M

P 97x   P 97C   P 100F   P 67x   P 248x   P 103B   P 99A   P 237B

P 338A   P 176x   P 083   P 181x   P 182D

ANTIQUE PERSIAN TILES. FINE ORIENTAL COLORING
AND ORIGINAL DESIGN.
WE MAKE PLAIN PERSIAN TO HARMONIZE.

PRECURSORS

THE MAIN STRANDS of the Art Deco style of the 1920s and 1930s were already discernible in Europe in the years leading up to the First World War, and this was also true of Britain. The Art Nouveau style that had swept through Europe at the turn of the century had become less dominant after the first decade of the twentieth century. Avant-garde movements such as German Expressionism, French Cubism, Italian Futurism, Russian Suprematism and English Vorticism were making their presence felt. The European artists associated with these new 'isms' shared an interest in deconstructing and abstracting the appearance of the world they painted or sculpted and their endeavours also had a profound influence on design and architecture in Britain.

Architects played a seminal role in bringing about a shift from Art Nouveau to Art Deco. Some of them were well-known foreign architects who had been commissioned to design and construct buildings in London. The French architect François Epinasse designed tailor-made headquarters for the Michelin Tyre Company on the Fulham Road, which opened in 1911. It was a commercial palace dedicated to the world of the motor-car with much use of faience and tiles in its exterior and interior decorations. Although the ornamentation of the Michelin Building is lavish, it is bolder and simpler than the unrestrained and intricate forms so often associated with Art Nouveau, and as such it can be regarded as a transitional building between Art Nouveau and Art Deco. For the tile enthusiast, the building's best features are its many tile panels showing famous motor races. These were celebrating a new and glamorous form of transport made quicker and easier through the use of the pneumatic tyre. François Epinasse called on the French firm Gilardoni Fils & Cie to design and produce the panels, which were made in Paris.

Another seminal building in London is Holland House in Bury Street in the City of London, designed by the leading Dutch architect H. P. Berlage. It was built for W. H. Muller & Co., a Dutch conglomerate involved in shipping, steel and mining, and it was opened in 1916. The façade is somewhat severe,

Opposite:
Catalogue page with tile designs by J. & W. Wade & Co., 1917, showing a variety of stylised floral and bird motifs. The simplification of the designs shows them as a transition from Art Nouveau to Art Deco.

11

Detail of one of the panels on the façade of the Michelin Building. Streamlining is already evident in the way the racing car has been depicted.

The façade of the Michelin Building, Fulham Road, London, is decorated with French tile panels showing early motor races, made by Gilardoni & Cie, Paris, 1909–11.

with rows of vertical rectangular windows clad in grey bluish-green faience made by the Dutch firm De Porceleyne Fles in Delft. However, the entrance lobby is surprising – a visual treat foreshadowing the splendours of Art Deco architecture. The Dutch abstract painter Bart van der Leck (a founder member of the famous Dutch De Stijl group) was initially involved with the decoration and colour scheme. The walls are made of white-glazed brick enlivened with horizontal bands of yellow relief tiles with abstract designs. Thin decorative strips of tile separate every two horizontal rows of glazed brick, and abstract white faience decorations embellish the top ends of the bevelled wall corners. The ceiling is divided into square compartments by steel beams and ornately decorated with abstract mosaic designs that are echoed by the square tile

arrangements of the floor. The faceted diamond-shaped glass lights hanging from the ceiling are in tune with the decor of this highly remarkable entrance hall, which still stands today as an important precursor to the Art Deco interior design of the inter-war period.

London was not the only place in Britain to see the early signs of Art Deco in commercial and domestic architecture. The architect Edgar Wood, from Middleton near Manchester, had become well known locally by the beginning of the twentieth century and was involved with some ground-breaking commissions just before and during the First World War. Wood also had dealings with the Manchester tile and pottery firm Pilkington's and designed the exhibition stand that the firm used at the Franco-British Exhibition in London in 1908. His use of tiles on the exterior of the stand shows a creative interplay of chevron designs that was to become such a major design feature of Art Deco tile design. He used similar tiled chevron patterns on the façade of a parade of shops in Middleton that he designed in 1908. In 1914–16 he built his own house in Hale just outside Manchester. The house is built of traditional brick but it has a flat roof and a concave façade with stone dressings. On the

The entrance hall of Holland House in London, designed by the Dutch architect H. P. Berlage and opened in 1916, illustrated in *Examples of Delft Tiles & Faience*, published by A. Bell & Co. Ltd, Northampton, c. 1930.

ENTRANCE, HOLLAND HOUSE, BURY STREET, LONDON, E.C.
White glazed Brick, with Delft strips and strings, and mosaic panels to ceiling.

The Pilkington's Pavilion at the 1908 Franco-British Exhibition in London. Designed by Edgar Wood and illustrated in the *Franco-British Exhibition Illustrated Review*, Chatto & Windus, London, 1908.

façade above the front door is a large panel of striking patterned tiles with a strong zigzag design worthy of the best Art Deco examples. This zigzag design is also echoed in the decoration of the front door.

Art Deco architecture of the 1920s and 1930s is often associated with cinemas, but an unusual very early example could be found in Sheffield until it burned down in 1982. It was called the Electra Palace and used to stand in Fitzalan Square in the city centre. It was opened

The exotic façade of the Electra Palace, constructed of Burmantofts Marmo and built in 1910–11. Formerly at Fitzalan Square in Sheffield, it burned down in 1982.

Opposite far left: The façade of Edgar Wood's own house in Hale near Manchester, built in 1914–16. The strict geometry of the tile decorations foreshadows Art Deco design of the inter-war period.

Opposite: Detail of the zigzag tile design on the façade of Edgar Wood's house in Hale.

in 1911 and was designed by the architectural firm of Hickton & Farmer. It had an oriental style façade made of 'Marmo', a special type of faience made by the Leeds firm Burmantofts. The exoticism of this cinema building was remarked upon by the *Sheffield Daily Telegraph* of Friday, 10 February 1911 as 'Fifteenth Century Arabian Architecture, as seen in its eastern glory of detail and colour in Cairo'. Its whimsical façade was accentuated by horizontal bands of light and dark faience with Egyptian-style decorations at the top of the façade and a small sunburst motif over the entrance. All of these were design elements that would become popular in later Art Deco architecture and designs.

It was not only architecture that was affected. In the world of British product design there were also changes afoot. In 1915 the Design and Industries Association (DIA) was founded to improve standards of industrial design under the slogan 'Nothing need be ugly'. Its aim was to foster better co-operation between manufacturers, designers and retailers, and key people from these three areas were included in the group of founder members, such as the ceramics manufacturer Cyril Carter and the artist Harold Stabler, who a few years later would be working together in the ceramics firm Carter & Co.

Bringing contemporary artists closer to the world of commerce and industry was also the main motivation of an unusual venture in interior decoration and product design – the founding of the Omega Workshops in London in 1913. These groups were set up by the art critic and artist Roger Fry and included members of the Bloomsbury Group such as Duncan Grant and Vanessa Bell, but there was also the artist Wyndham Lewis, who after an early disagreement with Fry left Omega and founded the radical art movement Vorticism. The Omega Workshops made furniture, textiles and also pottery and tiles decorated with colourful abstract designs. Because of the First World War the economic climate in which they operated was difficult and they had to close Omega in 1919, but it left a legacy. During the period while Omega was in business, Fry established links with the firm Carter & Co. in Poole and undertook some experimental work in making pottery at their factory. This exposure to the work of avant-garde artists would bear fruit in the inter-war period when Carter & Co. became one of the most innovative ceramic firms in Europe and became well known for using highly qualified artists to design and produce Art Deco pottery and tiles.

The various developments in design and architecture just outlined also began to have an impact on what was happening in the wider commercial tile world. This is evident in what was on show in the trade catalogues of the period such as the *Architect's Standard Catalogues* for 1914–17. One example is the tile manufacturer J. & W. Wade & Co., who among their examples of decorative tiles also advertised tiled dados. Many of the dados that were illustrated show that the influence of Art Nouveau still lingered on, but there were also examples where more simplicity was in evidence. Dados were being made of plain tiles with the occasional decorative inset, which would become the norm in the 1920s and 1930s. The same applied to Wade's decorative tiles. Gone was the Art Nouveau whiplash with its sinuous linear design; what was now prominent was motifs that were more restrained and showed an underlying geometric sense of abstraction, heralding the days of Art Deco tile design of the inter-war period.

Opposite:
Catalogue page
with tiled dados by
J. & W. Wade & Co.,
1917, demonstrating
the waning of Art
Nouveau and the
introduction of
more simple Art
Deco designs.

WALL AND FLOOR TILE SECTION 46

J. & W. WADE & CO.
FLAXMAN TILE WORKS
BURSLEM, ENG.

Telegrams: "WADES, BURSLEM"
Telephone: 341
A. B. C. Code. 5th Edition

D 488   D 489   D 490   D 491

D 492   D 493   D 494   D 495

TILE DADOS WHICH CAN BE SUPPLIED
GUELPH OR ENAMEL FINISH

SCALE: ONE INCH TO FOOT

DECORATION
TECHNIQUES

A FTER THE First World War there was a more pragmatic approach to tile making, brought on by the changed economic circumstances of the post-war world and the different demands of builders and architects. This was accompanied by improvements in technology, which led to increasing mechanisation in the tile industry. Electric tile presses were introduced, replacing the hand-operated or steam presses, and there was the development of the continuous kiln, sometimes called a 'tunnel kiln', which was more energy-efficient and reliable than the traditional bottle kiln.

The inter-war period also saw the development of modernism in architecture and although there was still a big demand for tiles, particularly in the burgeoning housing industry, the taste had veered towards plain tiles rather than decorated ones. The demand for tiles was boosted by the growing housing industry. The Housing and Town Planning Act of 1919, devised by Christopher Addison, offered a partnership between the state and local authorities to build increasing numbers of council houses, which were built with amenities such as tiled bathrooms and tiled fireplaces. In the 1930s private developers and builders took advantage of low interest rates, low land costs and a lowering of the cost of materials to build affordable homes for the middle classes, of which the semi-detached house became the most popular type of the period. This was the target market for the tiling schemes in the tile company catalogues of the 1930s.

The fashion for decorative tiles had changed dramatically. In the preceding Victorian and Edwardian ages, the use of decorative tiles over extended wall areas was common, but they were now used as occasional insets among a mass of plain tiles, which were often decorated with matt or mottled glazes. These so-called 'eggshell' glazes developed in the 1920s and 1930s were not always in pastel colours but could be very bright and intense, like the popular orange vermilion, which was striking when contrasted with black. Such bright glazes were achieved by adding uranium oxide (which can be slightly radioactive) to the glaze components.

The physical format of tiles changed as well. Although the traditional standard size of tiles of 6x6 inches was still used, there was an increasing

Opposite:
Art Deco tile
with an abstract
design tube-lined
with black slip and
decorated with
a mottled orange
eggshell glaze.
Made by
Pilkington's,
c. 1930.

Detail of an Art Deco faience block for use in a fireplace, with matt and mottled glazes. The ranges of orange and brown colours were much in demand during the 1920s and 1930s.

preference for smaller sizes such 6x3 inches, 4x4 inches and 4x2 inches. There were also tile strips (often with simple decorations) measuring 6x1 inches, or even very thin ones of 6x0.5 inches.

Close examination of a tile or piece of faience will reveal how it was made and decorated. There were a number of different manufacturing techniques such as dust pressing, cloisonné, press moulding, and slip casting. The decoration on the surface of the tile body was carried out with materials such as clay slip, ceramic pigments and coloured glazes, and, since fewer decorative tiles were made as opposed to plain ones, it again became feasible to decorate tiles by hand with techniques such as tube-lining, stencilling and hand painting.

The manufacture of tiles made from dust clay is dependent on the technique of dust pressing, which was invented in 1840 by Richard Prosser. This had led to the mass production of tiles in the Victorian and Edwardian ages, and involved the use of specially prepared dust clay (usually white) with a low moisture content, which was compacted under great force in a metal die in a large screw press. The low moisture content meant that the tiles needed less drying time than tiles cut from damp plastic clay, and they also tended to warp less during drying and firing.

One of the great advantages of the dust-pressing method was that it simplified the production of tiles with relief decorations by using a metal mould with an intaglio motif (design in reverse) at the bottom of the press. In this way the tile and the relief decoration were made in one single operation. With dust-pressed Art Deco tiles it became the norm to press tiles in metal moulds with simple linear designs in reverse, which, after pressing, stood out as raised lines on the surface. After the first firing (biscuit firing) the tile would be covered with translucent glazes, which were prevented from running into one other by the network of raised lines on the surface of the tile. A variation of this process was to create machine-pressed tiles with shallow relief decorations accentuated by raised areas lying on the tile surface. The firm of H. & R. Johnson used the dust-pressed technique to create some beautiful floral Art Deco tiles in the 1920s.

The cloisonné technique was a process where raised lines were created on the surface of the tile by pressing plastic clay (ordinary malleable clay) into metal or plaster moulds. When the tile was lifted away from the mould, ridges delineated the design. The tile was then fired and the hollow areas between the lines were filled with different coloured glazes. This process was normally used for tiles with more intricate designs, where the line work

Page from a Bell & Co. catalogue of about 1930, showing tiles of different sizes made by the Dutch firm De Porceleyne Fles. The square pictorial tiles are the 4-inch format popular at that time.

21

needed to be more delicate than that of dust-pressed tiles. The cloisonné technique is not associated with English tile makers and was the speciality of Dutch firms such as De Porceleyne Fles in Delft, who would market their tiles in England via designated importers such as Bell & Co. in Northampton.

Press moulding was a method used to produce blocks of architectural faience using malleable clay, which was pushed by hand into large plaster moulds with intaglio relief designs. After a period of drying, the clay slab with its relief decoration on the surface was tipped out and left to dry for a further

Dust-pressed floral tile with machine-pressed raised white lines and the moulded areas in shallow relief and counter relief. Made by H. & R. Johnson, 1926.

Plastic clay cloisonné tile made by De Porceleyne Fles factory in Delft, c. 1930. The raised lines delineate the landscape motifs and the areas between the lines are filled with matt crystalline glazes.

period. If details needed to be made sharper, or if undercutting was required, the decoration could be worked on further by hand. The faience block could be fired before glazing or the glaze could be applied to the dry but unfired clay. Faience for exteriors was glazed with special monochrome or polychrome glazes developed for outdoor use. Complex figurative designs had to be made in several parts as there is a physical limit to how big a single section of clay can be, and section joints can often be seen running through the overall finished design in larger pieces.

Tiles were also slip-cast in plaster moulds. This method was mainly reserved for tile strips measuring 6x1 inches with simple line or relief designs. Liquid clay or slip was poured into a plaster mould and left to settle. Once the mould had absorbed most of the water, the top section was lifted and the tile tipped out for further drying. The firm of Minton made tiles using this method.

Hand decoration techniques fall into four categories: tube-lining, hand painting, stencilling and lustre. Tube-lining involved the piping of lines on to the surface of a dust-pressed biscuit tile much in the way that a cook ices a cake. A small bag with a nozzle at the end filled with liquid clay was used to pipe thin lines on to the surface of the tile to make a pattern or design. To ensure a close resemblance to the original design, the outline of what was to be tube-lined was transferred to the surface of the tile by use of a transfer. This was usually a piece of paper with the lines of the design pricked through; this was laid on the tile and some charcoal was brushed through the holes to leave a faint impression on the tile as a guide for the person doing the tube-lining. When finished, the slip lines could be burned on to the biscuit by giving the tile another firing before the glazing process, or the slip lines and the coloured glazes could be fired together.

Tube-lining could be done with dark- or light-coloured slip and factory workbooks with original tile designs often have precise written instructions on how a particular design was to be produced and what kind of glazes were to be used. The glazes were added between the lines, which acted as barriers to stop the glazes from running into each other. The tube-line method is characterised by lines and dots of clay, which form thicker areas

Press-moulded faience block made from plastic clay, with a floral design in high relief painted with matt glazes. Detail from the ornamental faience doorway of the former J. & J. Shaw's furniture store in New Wakefield Street, Manchester, installed in 1924.

A hand-painted abstract Art Deco design for a 4x4-inch tile dated '10-3-32', in a Pilkington's factory design book. According to the instructions written below the design, it was to be tube-lined with white slip and decorated with mottled eggshell glazes.

where lines intersect or change direction, or where the tile decorator paused momentarily, which adds an attractive hand-made look to this type of decoration that is absent from tiles with dust-pressed raised lines. The firm of Pilkington's made tube-lined Art Deco tiles something of a speciality.

Hand painting can be carried out under the glaze or on the glaze. In the case of under-glaze painting, high temperature colours are required as they need to be fired at the same temperature as the clear transparent glaze, which is applied over the painted design. Over-glaze painting is carried out with so-called enamel colours, which have the advantage of a greater colour range than can be used with under-glaze painting. Enamels are fixed to the already fired glazed tile at a lower temperature. However, over-glaze enamels are prone to wear as there is no glaze to act as a protective covering. There is, however, a third way, which is known as in-glaze painting, and this became a noted technique of the firm of Carter in Poole.

Detail of a hand-painted Carter & Co. tile with a design by Dora Batty, showing the nursery rhyme 'Little Bo Peep', c. 1935. The sure and deft brushstrokes made by the tile decorator can clearly be seen.

With in-glaze painting the pigment is applied on to the raw unfired glaze. The glaze is usually a creamy white one and the process was not unlike the traditional delftware technique practised in Holland. Once the painting on the unfired glaze has been completed, the glaze and the painted pigments are fired, which makes the pigment sink into the glaze and become an indelible part of it.

Stencilling is usually executed over the glaze. Stencils can be made from stiff waxed sheets of paper or thin sheets of zinc or copper. When only one colour is required, one stencil is needed. If more colours are needed, separate stencils must be cut for each extra colour. A design is cut into the stencil and what has been cut away will show as a flat area of colour on the tile. The stencil is placed on the tile and the pigment is applied by means of dabbing with a short-haired brush, but the aerograph method of blowing the pigment on to the tile in the form of fine spray was also used. Some strikingly good Art Deco tiles were made using this method by the firm of Dunsmore in London. The stencil technique can also be used in conjunction with hand painting. Carter & Co. produced stencilled tiles that were 'finished' by adding hand-painted contour lines.

Tile with a fluently
painted fish
expressing
agility and rapid
movement,
executed by
the artist
Polly Brace for
Dunsmore, c. 1930.

Tile with a
stencilled
decoration
showing one of
the signs of the
zodiac (Aquarius),
designed by
Polly Brace for
Dunsmore, c. 1930.

Lustre tiles were also made, but their production is not as common as the other decoration techniques described above. The application of lustre is a highly specialised branch of tile ornamentation and it is costly because of the components involved. Metallic oxides such as copper or silver were dissolved other glaze components. Special ingredients such as sulphur were added to act as reducing agents. The tiles were fired in a kiln, where a reducing atmosphere could be achieved (which means that there is no oxygen present). This was done by sealing the kiln after it had been fired up to its top temperature.

Tile with a stencilled decoration and some elements of hand painting, designed by E. E. Stickland and made by Carter & Co., c. 1935. The black lines of the turkey and the pink lines around the clouds have been painted by hand to accentuate the stencilled areas.

Four small copper lustre tiles arranged in a diamond shape, originally used as an inset in a slabbed fireplace, c. 1930.

Combustible material, such as thin brushwood or wood shavings, was introduced through a small hole that would immediately be sealed again. The wood would ignite and be forced to burn and so use up any oxygen that was in the kiln. This reduced atmosphere would help to create a thin film of metal on the tiles that, if successful, would have iridescent effects. In inter-war housing, small lustre tiles were made as decorative insets in fireplaces, but sometimes whole fireplaces were constructed of lustre tiles for the top end of the market.

The range of methods and techniques outlined meant that inter-war tile manufacturers had the resources and skills to make an interesting range of decorative tiles and faience to augment the vast production of plain tiles.

RICHARDS
TUBELINED INSETS

4 x 4'   T 119/D1

T 101/D1

T 102/D1

T 120/D4   4

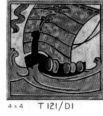

4 x 4   T 121/D1

T 96/D1

T 122/D1

T 55/D2

4 x 4
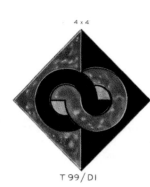

T 99/D1

8 x 8'

T 16/D1

4 x 4'

T 123/D1

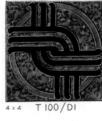

4 x 4   T 100/D1

T 82/D1

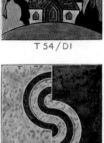

T 54/D1

T 74/D2

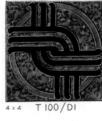

4 x 4   T 75/D1

T 98/D1

T 97/D1

T 79/D3

MANUFACTURERS AND DESIGNERS

TILE MANUFACTURERS responded positively to the new fashion for Art Deco and the subsequent demand for tiles in that style. Firms such as Carter & Co. in Poole; Maw & Co. in Jackfield near Ironbridge; Pilkington's Tile & Pottery Company at Clifton Junction near Manchester; Candy & Co. Ltd in Newton Abbot; and H. & R. Johnson, Richards Tiles and Minton, Hollins & Co. in Stoke-on-Trent, all made Art Deco tiles designed either by in-house designers or using designs commissioned from freelance artists. There were also small businesses such as Packard & Ord in Hungerford and Dunsmore in London who specialised in tile decoration only and bought ready made tile blanks from larger firms. It is also interesting to see how during the inter-war period women designers came to the fore in the tile industry, such as Truda Adams (later Carter) and Dora Batty, who designed for Carter & Co., Sylvia Packard and Rosalind Ord at Packard & Ord, and Polly Brace at Dunsmore. Previously their role had been largely one of executing the designs created by men, but they were now active as highly qualified designers in their own right who had been to art schools such as the Central School of Art or the Royal College of Art.

In Stoke-on-Trent there were several major firms making Art Deco tiles. H. & R. Johnson produced a good range for every kind of use. Company catalogues of the 1930s show a broad spread of designs that range from the semi-figurative to the completely abstract. The firm operated from the Highgate Tile Works in Tunstall and the Eastwood Tile Works in Hanley, which they had acquired when they bought out Sherwin & Cotton in 1911. They served the home market in the United Kingdom but also had a thriving export business that extended as far as South America. In the 1920s they made some well-designed floral Art Deco tiles in a 6-inch format, which were dust-pressed in the so-called 'white-line' technique, where the design lay as raised lines on the surface, which was then decorated with coloured translucent glazes. In the 1930s they produced abstract and semi-abstract tube-lined tiles with bold Art Deco designs decorated with strongly coloured glazes.

Opposite:
Page from a Richards Tiles catalogue dated 1936. It shows a fine range of semi-figurative and abstract tube-lined Art Deco tiles.

Right: Dust-pressed tile with tube-lined abstract Art Deco relief designs, decorated with colourful eggshell glazes. Made by H. & R. Johnson, 1926.

Also active in Stoke-on-Trent was Richards Tiles (until 1931 they had been know as Henry Richards Tile Company), who operated three factories, of which the Pinnox Works at Tunstall was the parent plant. By the 1930s they had become one of the major tile manufacturers in Britain, with offices in London and Glasgow. They made relief-moulded and tube-lined Art Deco tiles and they offered complete tiling schemes for butchers, fishmongers and other shops,

Right: Dust-pressed tile with a bold abstract Art Deco relief design, decorated with a single matt glaze that has settled as a darker colour in the lower areas. Made by H. & R. Johnson, c. 1930.

Far right: Dust-pressed tile with a semi-abstract floral design of a rose, painted with translucent glazes. Made by H. & R. Johnson, 1925.

and on the domestic front a fine range of bathroom suites. The style of their Art Deco tiles was wide and ranged from stylised landscapes and streamlined animal designs to bold geometrical abstract motifs.

Away from Stoke-on-Trent there was the well-established firm of Maw & Co. at Jackfield, who in the late 1920s and early 1930s made high-quality Art Deco tiles. Some show landscapes, but there was also an attractive series of tube-lined tiles with geometric abstract designs. They could be tube-lined in black or white slip and were painted with brightly coloured glazes. Some tiles even had part of the design highlighted with lustre, which gave them an extra visual appeal.

Semi-abstract Art Deco landscape tile with bold dynamic shapes. Made by Richards Tiles, c. 1935.

Pilkington's at Clifton Junction near Manchester had made their name during the late nineteenth and early twentieth centuries with the production of high-quality Arts and Crafts and Art Nouveau pottery and tiles, which had been designed by their own in-house designers and freelance artists and architects from outside. By the 1920s and 1930s their tile production had somewhat lost this high-profile image, although they still produced interesting figurative and abstract tube-lined tiles. Design books of the inter-war period have survived with original art work that shows hand-drawn and hand-coloured tiles with written annotations about production and decoration processes, and much can be learned from them. For example, they give the precise date when a particular tile design was made, what kind of tile body was used, whether it was

Far left:
A strikingly simple landscape tile, tube-lined in black and set within a circular border highlighted with gold lustre. Made by Maw & Co., c. 1923

Left: Tube-lined abstract Art Deco tile made by Maw & Co., c. 1930. The outlines of the design have been accentuated with gold lustre.

meant to be executed in black or white slip, and the various coloured eggshell glazes used in the decoration. With all this information to hand it is possible to follow a particular Art Deco tile design through from its inception to its use on the wall in a location such as a public house or a bathroom.

Candy & Co. Ltd in Newton Abbot produced some striking Art Deco tube-lined tiles with galleons in full sail, deer and pure abstract motifs. They made tiles for fireplaces that were assembled in their own slabbing shed, and their catalogues of the period show tiled dados and wall arrangements suitable for use in bathrooms.

The most interesting firm of the inter-war period in terms of the variety of tiles made and the range of artists employed was Carter's in Poole. It was a long-established firm, which, since the second half of the nineteenth

Tube-lined Art Deco border tile with red and black arrowheads. Made by Pilkington's, c. 1930.

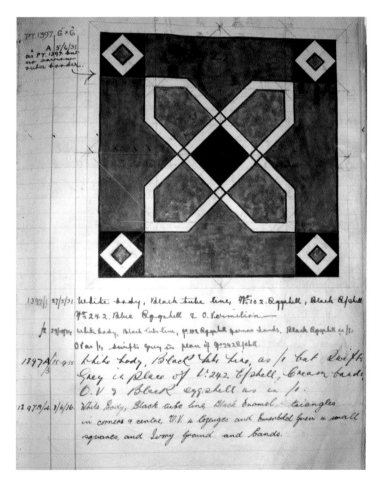

Hand-painted abstract Art Deco design no. 242 for a 6x6-inch tile dated '5-6-31' in a Pilkington's factory design book. It was to be tube-lined with black slip and decorated with vivid vermilion, blue and black eggshell glazes. More colour combinations are listed below the original instructions.

century, had been involved in large-scale production of wall and floor tiles, to which they added the manufacture of pottery and tableware at the end of the nineteenth century. The Carter family had run the business since it was founded by Jesse Carter in 1873, but in 1921 a new partnership was set up involving Cyril Carter, Harold Stabler and John Adams. Cyril Carter was the businessman and Harold Stabler and John Adams were trained designers and artists. Stabler and Adams also brought to the new partnership the artistic services of their wives, Truda Adams and Phoebe Stabler, trained artists in their own right. The firm therefore got a big artistic shot in the arm, which proved very advantageous for the design and making of pottery and tiles in the 1920s and 1930s. They raised their profile by taking part in national and international exhibitions and they were exhibitors at the famous *Exposition Internationale des Arts Décoratifs* in Paris in 1925, mentioned earlier, where they won a Diploma of Honour. Here the firm became acquainted with the work of the best European avant-garde designers, artist and architects. This was the catalyst that would lead to the dazzlingly bold designs and hand-painted patterns for their pottery and tiles of the 1920s and 1930s.

This involvement of artists with Carter's was not new. Artists from the Omega Workshops led by Roger Fry had already been involved with the firm. Furthermore, Carter's had also taken on the artist Joseph Roelants in 1914. A Belgian refugee from the First World War, he designed some of the first high-quality tiles, which went into production around 1917 with a series that was hand-painted on a tin glaze. The team of designers who worked for Carter's in the 1920s and 1930s – such as Truda Adams, Harold Stabler, Dora Batty, E. E. Stickland, A. Nickols, Edward Bawden and Reginald Till – were building on an already strong foundation.

Below: Hand-painted Carter & Co. tile, c. 1925, executed in an in-glaze technique with designs by Truda Adams (later Carter) (left), showing pomegranates. (Right) this semi-abstract 'African-style' floral design fits well into the Art Deco ethos of the period.

Truda Adams (she became known as Truda Carter when she divorced John Adams and married Cyril Carter in 1931) was responsible for many highly decorative floral and bird designs in the 1920s, which show the influence of modernist painting and French Art Deco design. Her floral tiles could be bold and semi-abstract but could also at times be minimalist, and some of her floral designs executed in dashes of bright colour are reminiscent of the colourful abstractions of Kandinsky. An interest in minimalist form can also be seen in a tile series called 'Water Birds' by Harold Stabler. Although the birds are recognisable in terms of their species (geese, ducks, gulls, etc.) their characteristic shape was pared down and simplified, which brought out their essentially aerodynamic lines. Background details such as clouds, land or water were indicated with a few swift dashes of the brush.

Not all the designers at Carter's were in-house. Dora N. Batty was an artist who undertook book illustration, poster and pottery design and she also taught at the London Central School of Art. For Carter's she created a series of designs in the early 1920s called 'Nursery Rhymes' and 'Nursery Toys' that were used on tiles and plates and seem to have been aimed specifically at the children's market. In Carter's catalogues they were advertised as having 'been very successfully used in fireplace surrounds and to add colour and interest to simple wall tiling schemes'. The designs were cheerful and painted in vivid colours and captured the figures of nursery rhyme characters and animals with playful yet precise linear definition.

E. E. Stickland and A. Nickols specialised in tile designs for single tiles and panels showing farmyard and dairy subjects. These were designed in the inter-war poster style of flat areas of stencilled colour accentuated by painted black lines. They worked very well as occasional insets in walls, where they

Below: Hand painted Carter & Co. tile, c. 1925, executed in an in-glaze technique with a design by Truda Adams of a spray of semi-abstract flowers.

Below right: Hand-painted Carter & Co. tile with a bird design by Harold Stabler, from the 'Water Birds' series, c. 1937.

HAND-PAINTED TILES

NR 6   NT 1

SP 2   WB 5

NR/6. One of a set of six Nursery Rhyme tiles from designs by Dora N. Batty. Painted on 5″× 5″ and 6″× 6″ tiles.
NT/1. One of a set of six Nursery Tiles from designs by Dora N. Batty. Painted on 5″× 5″ and 6″× 6″ tiles.
SP/2. One of a set of six Sporting Subjects from designs by Edward Bawden. Painted on 5″× 5″ and 6″× 6″ tiles.
WB/5. One of a set of six Water Bird tiles from designs by Harold Stabler. Painted on 5″× 5″ and 6″× 6″ tiles.
Sets NR, NT, SP and WB have each an appropriate intermediate tile for use with them.

Detail of a Carter & Co. catalogue of 1937, showing hand-painted tile designs by Dora N. Batty, Edward Bawden and Harold Stabler. These colourful designs epitomise the best of Carter's decorative tiles of the inter-war period.

would provide a splash of colour. Another interesting series was created by the artist Reginald Till, who designed a set of so-called 'Coloured Line Tiles'. They were playful semi-abstract line compositions to be executed in the same colour as the wall of plain tiles in which they were to be set, and were meant to be inserted at random to add interest to the wall. Their function was, to quote from a contemporary catalogue, to 'punctuate and inflect a wall of tiles as commas and full stops make readable a printed page'. The playfulness and energy conveyed by these hand-drawn linear designs bring to mind one of Paul Klee's famous dictums on art as 'taking a line for a walk'.

One of the last series of tiles made at Carter's in the inter-war period was designed by Harold Stabler for the London Underground. In the period 1937–9 he designed relief-moulded tiles for a number of new underground stations such as St John's Wood. There were eighteen different designs representing such things as the symbols of the Home Counties and famous London locations. They were covered in a single semi-matt cream-white glaze and usually have a little *S* at the bottom of the designs, which stands for Stabler. They were used as decorative insets among plain tiles of the same colour.

Section of a page of the Carter & Co. 1937 catalogue, showing hand-painted abstract linear tile designs by Reginald Till. They were designed to be insets in walls of plain tiles and were well suited for Art Deco interiors.

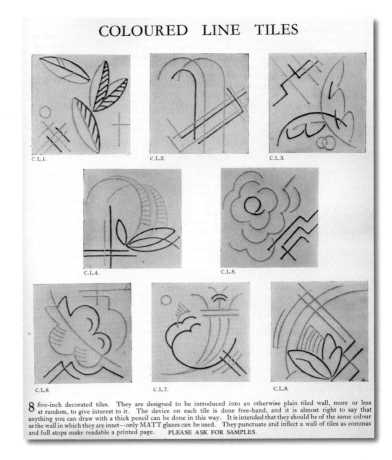

COLOURED LINE TILES

C.L.1.   C.L.2.   C.L.3.

C.L.4.   C.L.5.

C.L.6.   C.L.7.   C.L.8.

8 five-inch decorated tiles. They are designed to be introduced into an otherwise plain tiled wall, more or less at random, to give interest to it. The device on each tile is done free-hand, and it is almost right to say that anything you can draw with a thick pencil can be done in this way. It is intended that they should be of the same colour as the wall in which they are inset—only MATT glazes can be used. They punctuate and inflect a wall of tiles as commas and full stops make readable a printed page. PLEASE ASK FOR SAMPLES.

In addition to the big tile makers there were also small companies who were able to capture a corner of the market. One such firm, Dunsmore, did not make their own biscuit tiles but bought tile blanks from firms such as Woolliscroft and Minton in Stoke-on-Trent. Dunsmore Tiles was set up in the mid-1920s by Mary Brace (known as Polly) and Kathleen Pilsbury in Camden Hill, London. Most of the tiles were designed by Polly, who had trained at the Central School of Art. She specialised in fish, bird and animal designs executed either as handpaintings or in a technique combining handpainting and stencil. Her hand-painted tiles show great dexterity and skill and fluent handling of the brush. The stencilled and hand-painted tiles combine flat areas of colour with bold line work. One interesting series of designs depicting the signs of the zodiac was executed as stencils only, but the bold flat forms of the star signs clearly show the influence of Egyptian art which was popular at that time.

Panel of twelve stencilled tiles showing the signs of the zodiac, designed by Polly Brace for Dunsmore, 1928. The star signs Gemini and Aquarius in particular show the influence of Egyptian design, which was popular in the 1920s and early 1930s.

Another small tile venture was set up by Sylvia Packard and Rosalind Ord, who were both qualified art teachers. They had begun to decorate tiles in a small way in the early 1930s with tile blanks bought from Carter's in Poole, where their tiles were initially fired. As their reputations grew and more commissions came in, they decided to set up a formal partnership in 1936 under the name of Packard & Ord, which had its base in Hungerford, where they were joined by a third woman designer, Thea Bridges. They now had a kiln and could fire their own tiles, but they still had to buy ready-made blanks from firms such as Rhodes Tile Co. in Stoke-on-Trent. They therefore continued to be tile decorators only. Their hand-painted designs ranged from flowers, birds and animals to nursery rhyme subjects painted in a charming, free, simplified style that was very popular in the 1930s. One series of tiles known as 'Decorative Animals' stands out. They were painted by Rosalind Ord and show deftly painted animals such as hares, deer and dogs running along swiftly in a kind of streamlined style.

Hand-painted tile showing Little Miss Muffet, from the 'Nursery Rhymes' series made at Packard & Ord and painted by Thea Bridges in 1938.

When looked at as a whole, the tiles of the period 1920–40 show that there was a remarkable diversity of well-designed tiles executed in a range of techniques that made a significant contribution to the history of Art Deco design in Britain.

STYLES AND SUBJECT MATTER

THE INTERESTING RANGE OF STYLES and themes on Art Deco tiles came from many different sources in the history of art and design. Most of them were from the avant-garde art movements of the time such as the French Cubists, the Italian Futurists and the English Vorticists, but tile designs were also influenced by contemporary design movements such as the German Bauhaus and the Russian Constructivists, who favoured abstraction. Alongside this modernity, Art Deco inspiration was also drawn from the art and designs of ancient Egypt and South America and even African tribal art.

The use of abstract geometrical form became one of the most memorable features of Art Deco design. Pure abstract form that had no reference to the natural world had already been explored by a number of European painters. In particular, Mondrian and his fellow artists in the Dutch *De Stijl* group, founded in 1917, were important pioneers of abstract art and design. They pared down the shapes of the natural world to their basic geometric components and used strong primary colours (red, blue, yellow) and secondary colours (orange, green, purple) in combination with white and black. They had a marked influence on the German Bauhaus, whose students were taught to approach design from a standpoint of elementary form and colour. During the inter-war period the principles of Bauhaus design education also began to influence design education in Britain, so it is therefore not surprising to see Art Deco tiles with abstract motifs.

Abstract Art Deco tiles fall into two categories: tiles with static forms, and tiles with dynamic motifs. Tiles with static forms were usually composed of vertical and horizontal lines, which intersected to create a composition of interlocking squares and rectangles that were then filled with different colours. Tiles with dynamic motifs had intersecting diagonal lines and curves that created the suggestion of movement and jazzy shapes. Tiles with abstract motifs were also often grouped together to create zigzag and sunburst designs, and these were used to great effect as part of tiled fireplaces or above the main entrances of buildings.

Opposite: Detail of the colourful neo-Egyptian faience decorations on the façade of the Carlton Cinema, Islington, London, 1930. This shows several of the strong influences on Art Deco design: Egyptian, geometric, and a hint of Art Nouveau in the flower heads. See also page 49.

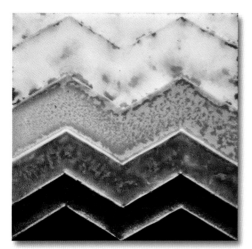

Tile made by Candy & Co. Ltd, with a tube-lined chevron design, c. 1930.

Another feature of Art Deco was the streamlined and aerodynamic forms that became so symbolic of the inter-war machine age. This had been explored earlier in the century in the painting and sculptures of the Italian Futurists, who had influenced the English rebel avant-garde group the Vorticists, founded in 1914, who experimented with similar themes. In design, it meant stripping form down to its bare essentials with shapes expressing speed, dynamism and motion. In tiles, it manifested itself by depicting streamlined birds in flight, sleek deer streaking along or the taut curved lines of billowing ships' sails.

The discovery of the tomb of Tutankhamun by Harold Carter in 1922 sparked off great interest among designers and architects at the time. The contents of the royal tomb, with its furniture, sculptures and jewellery and, above all, the mummy of the boy king wearing his famous golden mask, created a short-lived frenzy in inter-war art and design. Tiles and faience were also affected by this craze. Egyptian themes such as sphinxes appeared and lotus buds and flower motifs became popular design elements, particularly for the colourful architectural faience decorations on

Right: An unusual tile with a sunburst motif. Made by Godwin & Thynne, early 1920s.

Far right: Abstract relief-moulded Art Deco tile. Made by Candy & Co. Ltd, c. 1930.

cinemas in the 'Egyptian' style. The human figure was sometimes depicted on tiles in an Egyptian stylised way, with the torso seen straight on but the face and hips in profile and the arms outstretched.

Figurative scenes were also a prominent aspect of Art Deco tiles. Although abstract and streamlined forms are now often regarded as typical of the Art Deco movement, representational designs executed in a flat stylised way are in certain instances also regarded as Art Deco. After all, it is not what is represented but how the artist has used line, form and colour that make something Art Deco in style. Landscapes, for example, have long been established subjects in the history of art and design, but they were given strikingly new treatments in the 1920s and 1930s. Trees and buildings were reduced to their essential outlines and clouds

Landscape tile painted by Sylvia Packard, c. 1937. The highly stylised landscape with the sleek shape of the fast running deer is fashionably streamlined.

Tile with line relief and mottled glazes, depicting a streamlined stag, early 1920s. Made by Candy & Co. Ltd.

41

became a collection of circular shapes. Perspective was almost eliminated to make the scene look flat and strong colours were used to accentuate different parts of the composition. This can also be seen on tiles and pottery and was used to great effect by well-known ceramic artists of the time such as Susie Cooper and Clarice Cliff. Their Art Deco landscapes became very popular with the wider public and also influenced tile design of the period.

Other themes that were much demanded by customers were nursery rhymes, fairy tales and farmyard scenes. These tiles were executed in a flat, stylised and simplified way with bright colours and were aimed at children. The expansion of the housing industry in the inter-war period saw many middle-class and upper-middle-class houses being built with sufficient space for special

A design for a faience panel showing an Egyptian goddess on a throne, executed in bright colours. The actual panel based on this design was on the exterior of the exhibition stand of the faience manufacturer Shaws of Darwen at the the Building Trades Exhibition, Olympia, London, 1932.

Stylised tube-lined landscape with buildings. Made by Richards Tiles, c. 1935.

rooms to be set aside as nurseries. In previous times nurseries had been decorated with wallpaper and tiles that had an educational purpose, but in the inter-war period the balance changed so that rooms for children became places that were fun to be in rather than merely instructive, as was often the case in Victorian and Edwardian times. Tiles

designed with scenes for children fitted very well into this kind of environment and that is why manufacturers such as Carter & Co. and tile decorators such as Sylvia Packard produced tiles with such themes to satisfy a particular market demand.

Above left: Hand-painted 'Nursery Rhyme' tile showing Little Miss Muffet, based on a design by Dora Batty. Made by Carter & Co., c. 1925.

Above: Hand-painted 'Nursery Rhyme' tile showing 'This Little Pig Went to Market'. Made by Ashtead Potters Ltd, c. 1925. The little zigzag motifs confirm its Art Deco credentials.

Tile panel made by Carter & Co. for the front of the W. H. Smith bookshop in Llandudno, c. 1930. The industrial harbour scene with an ocean liner, cranes and smoking chimneys is classic 1930s Art Deco. Eric Gill designed the font.

Tile panel at West Kirby Residential School in West Kirby, Wirral, with a scene of children listening to a story, based on a book illustration by Henriette Willebeek Le Mair. Made by Doulton, c. 1945.

Tiles or faience panels with fairy tales and nursery rhymes were sometimes specially commissioned for particular locations. One example is the faience panels showing scenes and characters from the stories of Hans Christian Andersen placed in the lunettes above the windows of the flats of the Sidney Street Estate behind St Pancras Station in London. They were commissioned by the St Pancras Home Improvement Society and were designed by the sculptor Gilbert Bayes at the beginning of the 1930s, intended to add a splash of colour and informality to the newly built housing estate. Bayes chose four Andersen tales – 'The Little Mermaid', 'The Wild Swans', 'The Soldier and the Princess' (see contents page image) and 'The Swineherd' – as decorations for the lunettes above the windows facing the large courtyard, and there was also a faience clock depicting small figures personifying the four seasons. The panels were made by Doulton & Co. and decorated with durable semi-matt coloured glazes. They have withstood the test of time well and can still be admired today.

If the Gilbert Bayes panels were for use on the exterior of buildings, tile panels with children's themes were also used inside hospitals and convalescent homes, where they brightened the long days. An example still extant is at West Kirby Residential School in the Wirral, which used to be a convalescent home for children from Liverpool. Benefactors endowed beds for children, which were marked by tile panels on the wall above the heads of the beds. The panels showed children playing and engaging in games. Several of them were based on pictures by the Dutch book illustrator Henriette Willebeek Le Mair, created in 1925, although the

In·Memory·of·MARY·ELIZABETH·NICKSON·and ETHEL·MARY·GREEN·her·daughter·of·Caldy·1943·

panels were made at a later date. The beds are no longer there, but the panels have survived and are still treasured and looked after.

Hand-painted tile from Carter's 'Sporting' series, designed by Edward Bawden, depicting punting on the river, c. 1935.

Another theme in Art Deco tiles was sporting subjects. Outdoor pursuits and leisure became increasingly important to the various classes in society in the inter-war period. Shooting, sailing and horse riding for the upper classes; hiking, swimming, golf and taking the car for a spin for the middle classes; and fishing, cycling, boating and football for the lower classes, were activities with which to fill increasing leisure time. This was all reflected on inter-war tiles. Edward Bawden, for example, designed a series of tiles for Carter & Co. in the 1920s showing a whole range of leisure pursuits, executed in a simplified and comic way and offering an affectionate portrayal of British outdoor life.

Tiles with sporting subjects were occasionally commissioned for specific locations. An intriguing example is the gentlemen's toilet of the the Sportsman pub in Huddersfield. It was built in the 1930s and customers who felt the need to 'spend a penny' could admire panels depicting such sporting activities as sailing, shooting, horse racing, fishing and football. The panel depicting football is particularly interesting as it shows a ball, football boots and a football shirt lying near a goalpost. The shirt is in the blue-and-white colours of the local Huddersfield team, which strengthens the idea that these panels were a special commission. All the various sporting scenes stretch across two 6-inch tiles and were executed in a black tube-line accentuated with bright translucent glazes.

Panel of two tiles with a slip-trailed design of football sports kit in the gentlemen's toilet of the Sportsman pub in Huddersfield, c. 1930.

ARCHITECTURAL APPLICATIONS

BRITAIN is not a country where we find much real Art Deco architecture. There was not a great deal built in the first place and over the years some fine examples have been lost through demolition. There are now relatively few buildings of the standard of the Hoover Building in Perivale, London, that can be matched with the Art Deco buildings of Europe and America. There were other important inter-war buildings that were constructed in a modernist style, such as the Berlei lingerie factory in Slough (now demolished), but, despite its ultra-sleek lines and plain faience cladding, it was not an Art Deco building. So what is the difference between Art Deco and modernism? The term 'modernism' in architecture conjures up white rendered walls, flat roofs, metal-framed windows and curved glass corners. Art Deco architecture also often possesses these qualities, but with prominent and sometimes flashy ornamentation. Modernism had the motto 'Less is more' and excessive ornament was frowned upon, as can be seen in the iconic Bauhaus building (1925) in Dessau, the work of Walter Gropius, who was one of the giants of the modern movement in architecture. The Bauhaus building was a serious exercise in developing new ways of constructing and articulating functional space based on carefully devised architectural theories. Another great modernist architect, the Frenchman Le Corbusier, entertained similar ideas. True Art Deco architecture is different. It can look modern in style but its decoration is a vital and essential part of it. This can be in the form of wrought iron, coloured leaded glass or colourful tiles and faience, but, whatever it is, it is the ornamentation that makes buildings really look Art Deco.

The most striking examples of Art Deco tiling and faience can be seen on the façades of such buildings as inter-war cinemas, offices, department stores and factories. Cinemas were very much buildings of their time and often show different aspects of the Art Deco style. Attention has already been drawn to the unusual and spectacular Electra Palace in Sheffield as an example of pre-Art Deco architecture, but in West Yorkshire there is also the Picture House Cinema in Castleford built in 1921. Although this building, clad in white-grey

Opposite:
The façade of St Olaf House, London, designed by H. S. Goodhart-Rendel in 1928–32. The gold-coloured faience decorations by Frank Dobson are impressive pieces of Art Deco relief sculpture.

faience, is not overtly Art Deco in style, it is decorated with fine tile panels representing classical figures denoting Greek drama and music, set against a ground of blue faience. The female figures are confidently executed and have a touch of stylised elegance and grace reminiscent of French Art Deco of the early 1920s.

But the Carlton Cinema on Essex Road in Islington, London, is proper Art Deco and truly eye-catching. It was designed by the architect George Coles, who specialised in theatre and cinema architecture, and whose work usually has the novelty factor. Hence we see exotic Chinese and Egyptian cinema designs, but also designs of a more modernist kind, as seen in the buildings of the Odeon

The strikingly modernist Berlei lingerie factory at Slough, designed by Sir John Brown, 1937. It was faced with plain faience made by Shaws of Darwen. The factory was demolished in 1982.

The Picture House in Castleford, 1921, with a classical figure holding a bowl of fruit and a mirror. The elegant stylised figure is typical of early 1920s Art Deco design.

chain. The Carlton Cinema is a glorious reincarnation of an Egyptian temple faced with colourful faience by the Hathern Station Brick and Terra Cotta Company. Its cream-white faience façade is liberally decorated with papyrus-bud capitals and lotus flowers and augmented with friezes featuring chevron patterns, and all executed in vibrant red, yellow, blue and green matt glazes.

A tremendous Art Deco office block is St Olaf House at Hay's Wharf next to London Bridge, designed by the architect Harry Stuart Goodhart-Rendel, 1928–32. It is a modernist steel-framed building, clad in white Portland stone, overlooking the river Thames, and was built as the headquarters for the Hay's Wharf Company. The most striking aspect is the river frontage, which is seven bays wide and is supported at ground level by

Detail of the façade of the neo-Egyptian Carlton cinema in Islington designed by George Coles, 1930.

Detail of the façade of St Olaf House, London. The treatment of the figure is bold and 'Cubistic'.

six evenly spaced black columns. The central three bays from the first to third floors are pierced by three tall, narrow windows surrounded by thirty-nine gold-coloured faience panels made by Doulton, and edged in black granite. The panels were designed by the British artist and sculptor Frank Dobson and depict scenes from the dockside under the headings of Capital, Labour and Commerce. The bold semi-abstract figures show an affinity with the figures of the French Cubist painter Fernand Léger and show that Art Deco decorations were often closely influenced by great contemporary artists and art movements.

Shops and department stores were also part of the Art Deco scene. To have an Art Deco façade showed that a place was modern and in the forefront of things, and it was also possible for existing shops to opt for a 'facelift'. For example, the inter-war faience manufacturer Shaws of Darwen could transform a traditional shop front into a striking Art Deco façade in a matter of weeks. Stores such as Burton and Woolworth opted for bold and modern façades in order to project a carefully designed, up-to-date corporate image. In the 1930s Woolworth had hundreds of stores throughout Britain and they even had their own construction company. One of their most striking stores was erected in Blackpool in 1938 on a prime site adjacent to Blackpool Tower. The store was given a skyscraper look and the whole façade clad in cream-white faience by Shaws of Darwen. Closer observation reveals neo-Egyptian design details such as stylised lotus flowers and also Art Deco zigzag motifs.

In the 1920s and 1930s new factory buildings sought more visual prominence and often used colourful tiles and faience to draw attention to themselves. Some were designed on a gigantic scale, such as the Firestone factory in Brentford and the Hoover Building in Perivale, both on the outskirts of London, or the India of Inchinnan factory built for the India Tyre & Rubber Co. near Glasgow. All three were decorated with coloured tiles and faience by

The tower of the Woolworth Building in Blackpool, 1938, clad in white faience. The stepped shape of the tower and the abstract and neo-Egyptian detailing are reminiscent of inter-war American skyscrapers.

Detail of the neo-Egyptian faience decorations on the Woolworth Building in Blackpool, showing lotus flowers and zigzag motifs.

Right: Detail of the main entrance of the Hoover Building, showing the stunning sunburst motif that is the defining feature of the main entrance.

Below: The imposing façade of the Hoover Building, Perivale, London, was designed in the early 1930s by Wallis, Gilbert & Partners. It is now one of the most iconic Art Deco buildings in Britain.

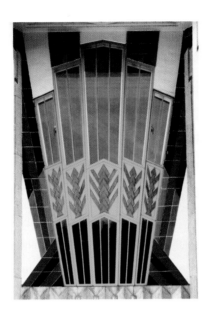

the firm Carter & Co. and were designed by Wallis, Gilbert & Partners, an architectural practice specialising in inter-war factory buildings. The factories were built on arterial roads near big cities and were meant to be seen by passing motorists. The simplicity of the façades and carefully located company names and logos above the main entrances enhanced by coloured tiles were designed to be remembered, and the Hoover factory (now owned by Tesco) is the most impressive of them all.

The building was constructed in the early 1930s for the American firm Hoover Ltd and it was given a long white-fronted façade punctuated by tall columns that gave it a faint Egyptian feel. The visual impact of the façade was further accentuated by vivid red, blue, green and black glazed ceramic tiles. Strong reds, greens and blues appear in the corners of the building and red stripes zigzag their way across the whole length of the façade. This use of colour was sensational in the predominantly drab surroundings of the early 1930s. The real glory is the main entrance, with sharply angled metal decorations on doors and windows, with a wonderful sunburst motif of coloured tiles, metal and glass above the door, which now makes it one of the most treasured Art Deco buildings in Britain. This is just as well, because since the 1980s some fine Art Deco factories have been demolished, of which the Firestone Building in Brentford has been one of the greatest losses. Also a sad loss was the Minimax fire-extinguisher factory in Feltham near Heathrow, of which now only the entrance propped up by steel beams remains.

The main entrance, with its red and blue faience, is all that remains of the once stunning Art Deco Minimax fire-extinguisher factory in London.

Art Deco tile panel with incised animals, designed by John Skeaping, on the exterior of Whitwood Mere Infants School, Castleford, Yorkshire, built in 1938–41.

A photograph showing 'slabbing' in process at the fireplace works of the Metal Agencies Co. Ltd in Bristol in 1937.

An Art Deco slabbed fireplace with matching wooden mantel in the Metal Agencies Co. Ltd catalogue of September 1937.

The " Failand "

Tiles and panels in the Art Deco style were also sometimes used in and on school buildings. A fine example still extant is Whitwood Mere Infants School, Castleford, in West Yorkshire, built between 1938 and 1941 and designed by the modernist architect Oliver Hill. On the exterior of the school below the windows are green tile panels with hand-incised decorations of running animals such as horses and deer to the design of John Skeaping and made at Carter's in Poole. The streamlined forms of the animals are reminiscent of some of the pottery designs of John Adams. The school closed in 1993 but it has been turned into a small business centre and the panels are maintained in good condition.

Art Deco tiles were also used in domestic architecture. Some semi-detached houses were built to look modern, with features such as flat roofs, rendered white walls, and metal-framed windows with Art Deco style leaded glass, but the majority of the semi-detached houses of the inter-war period were built in a comfortable Voysey mock-Tudor style, but that did not stop them having Art Deco decoration. Fireplaces and bathrooms were often 'jazzed up' with Art Deco tiles to make them look more 'modern'. Until the First World War, cast-iron fireplace grates set with decorative 6-inch tiles in a wooden or marble mantelpiece had been very common. In the inter-war period the use of open coal fires continued, but they were now burning in slabbed fireplaces that were made by attaching tiles to a concrete backing and were marketed as ready-made units that were easily installed. Contemporary hardware catalogues issued

A Bell's fireplace fitted with an electric fire, in a catalogue from around 1930, with a prominent sunburst motif in red and orange-yellow tiles. There are perforated tiles above the electric fire to assist the circulation of warm air.

by firms such as the Metal Agencies Co. Ltd in Bristol feature extensive selections of slabbed fireplaces for use in living rooms and bedrooms. They were usually made up of 4-inch tiles with matt mottled eggshell glazes and sometimes enlivened by insets of one or two ornamental tiles. It was also common to use plain tiles of different colours to create little Art Deco motifs at the top of the fireplace or at the bottom on either side of the grate.

Another firm that specialised in slabbed fireplaces was A. Bell & Co. in Northampton. They used tiles imported from the Netherlands made by the firm De Porceleyne Fles in Delft and their fireplaces are interesting to study

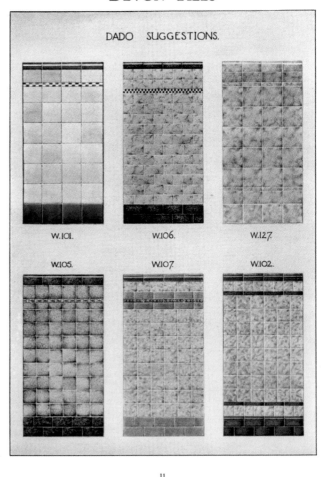

Page from a Candy & Co. Ltd catalogue of 1933 showing their Devon tile range for wall tiling. Tiled dados with mottled glazes and simple ornamental strips were popular for bathrooms.

because they show the twentieth-century changes in heating technology. Although open coal-burning fires were the norm in Britain, slabbed fireplaces with electric fires were also manufactured. With the completion of the National Grid in the 1920s, most homes had access to electricity and this new source of energy affected design. Fireplaces with electric fires sometimes showed 'sunburst' motifs, which acted both as striking Art Deco designs as well as suggesting actual rays of heat.

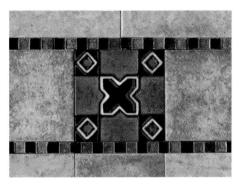

Bathrooms were also good places for the application of Art Deco tiling. There were subtle schemes with the walls covered in matt or mottled tiles with bands of lustre tiles at top and bottom augmented by coloured washbasins and shiny chrome towel rails. Or the design could be more obvious, with coloured tiles making up design features around the bath, washbasin and en-suite toilet, using horizontal and vertical bands of tiling as well as tiles with chevron motifs. Richards Tile Company created alluring names for these bathroom schemes, such as 'The Coral' or 'The Minaret', with which to tempt the middle-class house owner. Few of these installations have survived to the present day as fireplaces and bathrooms are particularly prone to refurbishment and renovation but tile catalogues issued by inter-war tile companies often show what these arrangements looked like.

Section of bathroom tiling with an arrangement of plain and decorative tiles made by Pilkington's, c. 1930. The plain tiles have matt mottled glazes and the decorative tiles and tile strips are tube-lined and glazed with the popular Art Deco colour combination of orange and black.

Bathroom decor called 'The Minaret' in a 1937 catalogue of Richards tiles. The differently coloured plain tiles have been used in an imaginative way to create a striking Art Deco bathroom interior.

COLLECTING

A RT DECO TILES are now eagerly sought after, and their striking and colourful designs make them prized items in many collections. They can be found at antique fairs and antique shops, obtained from architectural salvage firms or auction houses, or can be bought on eBay. Once a tile has been acquired, most collectors want the answers to some basic questions.

Detail of stall with twentieth-century tiles, including some fine Art Deco examples, at the annual Antique Tile Fair in Nottingham.

Who was the manufacturer? Who was the designer? When was it made? How was it made? What does the design represent? The answers can often be found by consulting specialist literature on tiles or by searching for internet websites featuring information on tiles.

The Art Deco tiles in your collection are worth studying closely. The front can reveal a lot about how it was decorated but the back can also be interesting, providing information about the manufacturer and the date of production. For example, many Art Deco tiles have the name or trademarks of the manufacturer stamped on the back, and sometimes even a date. There also publications that provide detailed information on tile backs and their markings.

Like any other antiques, tiles need to be looked after and there are a great many things a collector can do to display, store, conserve, photograph and catalogue tiles properly. How tiles are displayed is always a matter of personal taste and dependent on available space and financial means. Tiles can be effectively displayed on shelves and ledges or hung on the wall with wire or adhesive hangers. Some collectors prefer to frame their tiles in wooden or metal frames that give a homogenous and professional finish to the display.

Whatever display technique is adopted, it is more effective if it allows tiles to be arranged in groups to show specific types of subject matter, particular manufacturers or specific decoration techniques. Displaying tiles according to their subject matter can be visually very striking. It allows certain themes such as galleons with billowing sails, nursery rhymes and farmyard scenes to be displayed next to each other so that comparisons can be made. This approach also provides focus for what you can collect in future and you may well want to hunt

A collection of colourful 4-inch tube-lined Art Deco tiles made by Maw & Co., c. 1930.

The reverse of an H. & R. Johnson tile. It shows the name of the manufacturer at the top; the logo of the firm in the centre; the number 25 in the bottom left corner stands for 1925; no. 565 is a pattern number and no. 24 in the top right corner is probably a plate number.

Hand-painted nursery tile showing a hobby horse, based on a design by Dora Batty. Made at Carter & Co., c. 1925.

for a particular subject matter across a range of different manufactures and different designers.

Most collectors will eventually reach the point when they have more tiles than display space. Surplus tiles can be stored with care in strong cardboard or plastic boxes. The best method is to place them in an upright position with a piece of cardboard or thin polystyrene between each tile and keep them in a dry and accessible place. Multiple tiles are heavy, so store them in small boxes, which are easier to lift and handle. Do not store the boxes on top of each other as downward pressure could crack the tiles at the bottom of the pile.

Mark the box clearly on the outside with information about its content. This will avoid having to look through all the tiles when a particular example is required.

In order to care for a collection effectively it is also useful to follow certain essential guidelines that will help to preserve tiles in good condition as well as ensure they are displayed to their best advantage. When tiles are dirty and need to be cleaned, do not use ordinary tap water, which can cause salt growths and damage the tile by penetrating between the body and the glaze. Always use distilled water and a non-ionic detergent. Do not use abrasive cleaning pads, which can score the glaze, but use cotton-wool pads dipped in a cleaning solution. When the tile is clean, rinse it with distilled water and leave it to dry naturally. It can then be gently buffed with dry cotton wool. Organic stains can often be successfully removed by using hydrogen peroxide, which is commonly available from chemists. Soak the tile first in distilled water and apply a poultice soaked in hydrogen peroxide to the stained area and leave it to sit. Never use bleach or acid cleaners as they can the damage the clay body and the glaze. Tiles with a brown film caused by smoke deposits can be cleaned by wiping them with methylated spirit.

Tune-lined tile with a galleon and billowing sails. Made by Minton, Hollins & Co. in the late 1920s.

Tiles that have been covered with paint can easily be cleaned with paint stripper and a soft plastic scraper but care should be taken not to use metal implements as they may scratch the glaze surface. Tiles that have been used in damp areas and have absorbed salt from the wall on which they were fixed are often spoiled by a clump of white salt crystals. These can be removed by putting the tiles in a bath of deionised water and leaving them to soak, changing the water several times. The tiles should then be left to dry naturally before displaying them.

Be careful if you come across Art Deco tiles with bright orange-red glazes as these glazes were often derived from uranium oxide, which was used in the production of radioactive fuel and atomic weapons. Uranium glazes can emit beta rays and if checked with a Geiger counter may well produce a positive reading. However, in most instances the emission of radiation is very low and poses no threat to human health.

Creating a catalogue of your tiles is another interesting activity in tile collecting. Digital photography now makes it very easy to create an image that can be stored on your computer. Alternatively, if you have a scanner you will be able to make a colour scan of the tile. Once you have created an image

Relief-moulded tile made by Candy & Co. in the early 1920s, depicting a galleon in full sail.

Tube-lined tile showing a girl feeding a goose. Made by Richards Tiles, c. 1925.

give it an appropriate caption and store it in a clearly labelled folder. This will also allow you to share information with other collectors online. The World Wide Web has also become a mine of information about tiles and with the right search words a mass of interesting material about tiles is waiting to be discovered.

Responsible collectors are aware of the vanishing heritage of Art Deco tiles *in situ*. The demand for these tiles is high and they are sometimes removed unnecessarily or illegally from their original architectural locations. Such removal of Art Deco tiles not only robs us of already scarce tile installations, but inexpert removal often results in much breakage and damage. Many collectors are now members of groups and societies that not only serve the interests of collectors, but also encourage and support conservation.

Tube-lined tile depicting two geese. Made by Pilkington's, c. 1930.

FURTHER READING

Austwick, Jill and Brian. *The Decorated Tile*. Pitman, 1980.

Bayer, Patricia. *Art Deco Interiors –Decoration and Design Classics of the 1920s and 1930s*. Thames & Hudson, 1990.

Blanchett, Chris. *20th Century Decorative British Tiles*. Schiffer Publishing Ltd, 2006.

Duncan, Alistair. *Art Deco*. Thames & Hudson, 1988.

Greene, John. *Brightening the Long Day – Hospital Tile Pictures*. Tiles and Architectural Ceramics Society, 1987.

Lemmen, Hans van. *Tiles in Architecture*. Laurence King Publishing, 1993.

Lemmen, Hans van, and Blanchett, Chris. *20th Century Tiles*. Shire Publications, 1999.

Prescott-Walker, Robert. *Collecting Poole Pottery*. Francis Joseph Publications, 2000.

Stevenson, Greg. *Art Deco Ceramics*. Shire Publications, 2006.

Zaczek, Iain. *Essential Art Deco*. Parragon, 2000.

USEFUL WEBSITES

www.hansvanlemmen.co.uk

http://www.london-footprints.co.uk

www.pooleimages.co.uk

www.tilesoc.org.uk

INDEX